The One Minute Active Meditation Technique

belongs to:

____

Joy of the Journey!

Alannah Jantzen
May 2008.

by Alannah Jantzen

De-Mystify Meditation Series:

Book
The One Minute Active Meditation

Companion CD
One Minute Active Meditation
30 minute guided meditation

CD
Flow Spirit Flow
Toning, chants, drumming & rattle sounds
for Meditation & Journeywork

CD
Work of the Spirit
Drumming and Rattle sounds

De-Mystify Meditation

with the

One Minute Active Meditation

How to Unclutter Your Mind
And Connect with your Zest

Alannah Jantzen

Editing: Dawn Stewart, Gini Grey
CD recording, engineering and editing by Greg Dixon.
Cover photograph of meditation statue courtesy of Stella Perdios
Cover design and illustrations: Trevor Ploughman

Printed and bound in Canada by First Choice books, Victoria, B.C.

Published by Alannah Jantzen
Jantzen, Alannah H.
b. 1959 -

ISBN 978-0-9809430-0-9

1. Self-realization 2. Spirituality 3. Personal Growth

What people are saying:

Your CD is awesome, it is fresh, and a refreshing change from others I have heard. The sunshine in your voice is rejuvenating, love the part about the beach & curling up the toes. EXCELLENT JOB OF LOVE
Ashlie Delorme, Holistic Healer

This is an effortless program, powerfully thought provoking and practical; the One Minute Active Meditation book and CD is truly life enhancing. Alannah's light energy has flowed creatively through her, into her work. I really enjoyed it.
E.J. Lister – Author, Computer Consultant and Trainer

I have always failed at following meditation instructions because I couldn't understand how to digest all the instructions, then close my eyes and remember it all. Having the CD makes the process so much easier. Your book provides guidance, wisdom and practical techniques in a simple, easy to understand format that I think is unique.
Patricia Mason - Author

I laughed, felt a couple tears and it made me think! Also, I've used the One Minute Technique with my acting classes – it really works.
Wendy Carson, Actress

I LOVED IT! Alannah's suggestions for meditating are really helpful. I have an assortment of meditation tapes and CDs and this is now my favourite.
Dawn Stewart, Editor

Alannah Jantzen is a woman who can light up a room with her presence alone. I applaud her beautiful work in this book, using her life as a beacon for others.
Julie Blue - Recording Artist, Film Composer

Alannah's meditation recordings are fabulous - I am totally impressed and it is absolutely top notch.
Bob Burnham, Author - 101 Reasons Why You Must Write A Book

Having not taken any meditation courses before, I found it very interesting and the CD soooo relaxing. Suddenly I felt my face and shoulders just 'melt'. After I finished the session I was totally relaxed. Which was great because when my laptop cord caught on the door knob & sent my computer smashing down on the floor, I managed to just take a deep breath and walk away. Instant benefit!
Karen Eskilson, Property Manager

Alannah's book 'De-Mystify Meditation' does exactly what the title promises. In particular I find her approach to meditation allows me to access a wonderful source of creativity. Yet, her book goes beyond that; it also crystallizes her wide experience into a new way of thinking about ourselves and our relationship to others and the world.
Malcolm K. Smith Ph.D. President, Hands on Science

Thank you for this wonderful CD, it's beautiful and very gentle, like you. Nasrin Nemetzade, Translator

The De-Mystify Meditation book and CD are awesome. I am learning how and what all these mental push-ups are for. What I would not say to a friend, I having been saying to myself for years. Thank you Alannah for your insights and help towards a more creative and blissful life, I have spent 4 years learning, NOW I GET IT!
Hazel Barnbrook, Library Technician

I just read your book, not once, twice, but 3 times. Amazing! I love your stories, analogies and how you truly bring a deep level of understanding on life's journey, to all people. Also, the CD is excellent.
Dr. Sukhi Muker Chiropractor - Sunshine Life Studio

Alannah has found a way to make meditation simple, easy and quick for those with a busy schedule who want to clear their minds and calm their hearts. Her examples and stories make the book an enjoyable read and the CD guides you into your natural, peaceful state of wellbeing.
Gini Grey, Transformational Coach and Author - From Chaos to Calm and the CD - Create What You Want In Your Life.

Dedication:

For people, for you!

"And forget not the earth
loves to feel your bare feet
and the winds long
to play with your hair...."
author unknown

Acknowledgements:

With gratitude: To all my friends, family, storytellers, clients and angels, thank you.

Also to these special people for endless loving support, editing and grammar squad read through, sound engineering, marketing, book layout and joy of the journey, with special thanks for this project.

Tracey Spears
Greg Dixon,
Dawn Stewart
Stella Perdios
Susan Harris
Malcolm Smith
Irene Kobylkin-Somody
Patricia Mason
Bob Burnham
Ted Lister
Ashlie Delorme
Ruth Brothers
Trevor Ploughman
Saverio Autelitano
Gini Grey
Elaine Gibson

Chapters **Page**

Introduction		
1	Connect with your Zest	1
2	Make Friends with your Self	8
3	What is Meditation	17
4	Spiritual Pushups	29
5	Infinite Intelligence	35
6	Building the Foundation	42
7	Manifesting your Dreams	53
8	Excursions with the One Minute Active Meditation Technique	67
9	Nine Quick Steps	73
Conclusion		77
Further reading		79
About the Author		81

Introduction:

Hello dear reader! Simplify, simplify, simplify, that's what my clients all say they want. They also want a better life where they feel more in control and alive. This book is designed for you and for all the busy people who want to simplify meditation and your lives. No sitting for 30 minutes or an hour every day! One simple technique, not ten. Meditation can be something you integrate in to your daily life and do throughout your busy day. You can connect with the Infinite Intelligence, the creative wisdom and all knowing spirit presence within you, for calm, focus, clarity, creativity, and new inspiration to simplify your life - in just One Minute, anytime, anywhere! I devised the One Minute Active Meditation Technique through my own challenges and very busy life. I know this technique can help you in achieving your plans, goals and dreams.

In each chapter I present ideas on understanding how to connect with the Infinite Intelligence within. Feelings of zest and creativity, self-friendship, myths and truths of meditation – unclutter your mind! The benefits of meditation to take you through life's "Spiritual Pushups", understanding the Infinite Intelligence within that is the spark of life – the heart of our body. Then the "what and why" explanations for building a solid foundation for meditation. Also I have included a chapter on manifesting your dreams – taking the wondrous creative energy of the Infinite Intelligence within to bring your physical reality in to greater flow and success – with ease and grace. The chapter on Excursions with the One Minute Active Meditation is just that – go out and discover a new you! This book is meant to be used, so please scribble your ideas and a-hah! moments on the pages.

To further enhance your understanding and inner connection I produced a companion CD which is in the back of this book. The CD has both a guided meditation and the Ebook version of this book. The guided meditation can be played on any newer CD player as well as on your computer. On the CD I take you through Building the Foundation for meditation - un-cluttering your mind with the exquisite sounds of the Tibetan bowl, then guide you through a beautiful visualization of re-connecting with the light – the essence of your being. This is the same meditation as in the chapter Building the Foundation.

Truly, once you have built a strong foundation, then you can simply tune in and tune up throughout your day. You can use the One Minute Active Meditation technique, anytime, anywhere, eyes wide open or shut, and do it quickly, for health, focus, calm, creativity, and success. I assure you, with this technique it is simple, practical and literally, at your fingertips.

My hope is that you are inspired with my personal stories, life learning's, clients' experiences and years of spiritual healing to give you the courage and skills to embrace your life more fully. From the spark of life that created you, into the amazing, unique individual you now are – my sincere wish is that you come to know the infinite intelligence within you and that you learn how to co-create your life in beauty, truth and success with more ease and grace.

Wishing you joy of the journey,
Alannah Jantzen
March 2008

Chapter 1

CONNECT WITH YOUR ZEST

"May your choices
radiate from your heart, and
spring like glistening
blossoms in your eyes."
Alannah Jantzen

A double rainbow appeared right outside my window. Radiant, shimmering, stunning in the beauty of the light. I felt drenched in surreal beauty, awestruck in the moment.

My busy mind came to a complete stop. All the days' struggles ceased. The intense work paradigm shattered as my mind filled with wonder. Shallow breathing turned in to deep life nourishing breaths.

The sheer brilliance of the rainbow immediately re-aligned my perspective. The lesson I learned was:
"Stop, be present, feel the sensual beauty around you. This beauty creates your connection to the infinite presence of intelligence in all Creation and within you. This intelligence within you is the place where your strength and zest for life comes from."

What a great lesson! I hope that one is repeated as often as the hard ones.

You know, zest for life (that juicy inspiration filled place of wonder and curiosity), health, creativity, that place of deep inner connection to the purpose and meaning in life – these are true gifts to cherish. Some of my most creative and cherished moments occur when I am daydreaming or soaking in a bathtub. Also during that quiet connection place in meditation when I am clear and all the bubbles of new thoughts pop to the surface, or out in the forest, where nature hums a symphony of life. Yet, I also have times of clarity, creativity, and deep understanding by standing on a busy street and asking myself a question like – What is the next step in my life?

Every morning I have a little ritual to enhance the creativity and zesty feeling for my life. I hold my heart and say to myself – "Thank you! Please focus me on the amazing joyous journey of today. I willingly participate fully as you bring me clarity and ease of activities, flow, harmony, opportunities, synchronicities and prosperity. Thank you for all the wonderful relationships I have."

Sometimes it feels like a game! I watch for all the thoughts that pass through my mind, and notice the events that happen. I actively engage myself with the day's activities. Every day is the promise of great co-creative partnership inside of me and with everyone I meet.

You see, I am on a little mission. I want a better world, where people are kinder, communicate better, connect with their zest and the beauty and the spiritual intelligence within all living things. One on one, and within groups, my life has already made a difference. I intend to keep my promise to this infinite intelligence within me, to continue creating more joy and connection in the world. What a great work activity! Can you imagine your purpose in life, your work activity is to create joy and connection with people? It is what inspires me.

Inspiration comes in so many forms, and surely the light of a new day has got to be one of the most inspiring moments. Have you ever greeted the morning sun and really watched what happens? Participated in the immense energy of a new day dawning? The light filaments are like waves of joy in the heavens. There is a tremendous sense of awakening in the mind. You experience not only an exquisite artistic display, yet one of warmth and illumination. A new day has begun, full of possibilities. How do you participate with this life force, this gift?

A short story.

When I lived onbord a sailboat and sailed for 3 ½ years from San Francisco through the Panama Canal and then the Caribbean, opportunities for sunrise gazing were abundant as I had the 3am – 6am shift (by my choice!) Bleary eyed from the night's travel, however eerie, ghostly, calm or chaotic, the 4am stillness foretold the dawn. Sunrise was the new day and the light brought renewed hope and vigor.

One particular journey involved sailing along the Mexican coast (Pacific side) through an area called the Bay of Tehuantepec. It is south of Huatulco - we were heading to Costa Rica. This bay is notorious and can be a very dangerous body of water to traverse.

The Gulf of Tehauntepec is a natural isthmus - a valley that runs between mountain ranges and provides a funnel for weather in the Caribbean and the Gulf of Mexico to link with weather in the Pacific. The jungle valley is the lowest point and the mountains on each side form a funnel that intensifies any wind, just like a tube. It blows through and whips the water into a chaotic dance. Squirrelly – it's like hip-hop with Argentine Tango!

The Tehuantepec strategy is to circumnavigate the entire shore, which takes one and a half days, or take your chances and cut straight across – half your time. You really want to avoid the wrath - just ask the locals. Lots of fishermen die there. The Tehuantepec winds can blow 50+ knots and kick up 10 - 20 foot seas without any warning, in less than 10 minutes. Shallow bay, wind blowing against the tide creating waves that go straight up. Tangles of old traps, ship wrecks on the shore. We take our chances, decide to go for it and cut across. Remember that sailboats travel at about 6 miles per hour. At noon, one quarter of the way across that 125-mile stretch, the wind starts to dance on the water. Caught. Now the tests begin.

The wind is scary strong. Intense. We see winds of steady 50 knots and gusts of 65. For 10 hours it does not blow below 50. The spray scatters sheets of water for 20 plus yards beyond the boat. The sails tear, the bimini covering the cockpit rips off, we bounce up and down on 10-foot waves, heading back to shore. Like a slam-and-lurch slip-sliding affair. Salt water burning in our eyes and mouths. A long day, dusk falls. We start our shifts. No rest down below as we bounce up and down, yet, I am out of the howling winds. Near 4am – my shift, the winds calm. At 5am, the sky begins to lighten. At 5:30 am, the most beautiful serene warmth spreads over my dry salty face. I strip off my foul weather gear. I give thanks. I am alone, tired and relieved. Then, as always, quite happily sailing along on a calmer ocean, with the sun shining, I put on some beautiful music, breathe and shake off the fears of the night. My partner joins me at 6am and I yell "I want breakfast!" The light brings rays of hope and casts out the fears, a new day begins. I will always remember.

Over my years of being a therapist, healer, and life coach, helping people connect with themselves, I often wondered if they too had experiences of danger followed by the light, if they too would develop a deeper faith and illumination. The dominant dark habits people slip into when they get out of balance, their self-negating talk are like ghostly whispers transforming them into self-terrorizing organisms.

Opportunities to be overwhelmed in our crazy busy society feels like a footstep away sometimes. I've known sadness and depression and the place of beauty and joy, it has made me stronger. Fortunate to be curious and have the courage to do the unusual. Terrifying at times. Close brushes with physical death. Wonderful stories!

What I learned along the road is that all the stories and journeys have a big purpose. They are teachers. We are here on this planet learning. The difficult thoughts about ourselves, the harsh experiences, the stories we create through our fears, are the sand working in the oyster creating us as a beautiful pearl. Some people call themselves diamonds in the rough or a God/Goddess weaving new robes. However you see your life journey, remember your story will be an incredible teacher. The good news is that inside all that dark, heavy, self-absorbed side of the **"Story"** is the light. Just like the yin/yang symbol.

I learned along the way, that no one could be a better friend than I was to myself. No affirmations would ever replace the sheer physical, mental, emotional and spiritual depth of connecting within and finding the truth. (The truth is always warm and illuminating and the story of fear was cold and heavy.) When I hit a negative pocket, there is a place within me to go for comfort. Folks, it is **always** an inside job. You must build it and nurture it. No one can make you feel good about yourself. They can help you remember your beauty, yet you have to fall in love with you, before you can love anyone else. That is the beautiful source of manifesting all you desire. That is where this Infinite Intelligence within you manifests the creativity and zest to live your one wild precious life as a gift.

Now, when I walk down the street and notice all the stories, dramas, negative patterns, the hopelessness in peoples eyes, I have a choice. Either focus on what is good or get lost in that heavy dark drama. I choose to focus on what is good. I simply connect within with the One Minute Active

Meditation technique and create a song and say blessings. Have some fun. I remember how I started my day: "Please focus me on the amazing joyous journey of today." My new story and opportunity for a great experience can be one step away. I could flip the switch in someone's mind to a new perspective, by a smile or a crazy thought of joy. I could make a difference by simply being present and saying YES to life.

I want to share something with you, a little something I learned about saying YES to life. I'm notorious for making up simple songs and this one simply popped into my head after a yoga class. (Must be something about those awkward postures that tickle my funny bone.) I often feel that information is simply downloaded from this great data bank in the sky – my angels have certainly been busy over the years as I am firmly connected.

Here's a crazy little suggestion . . . Next time you are feeling a little blue or engaging in some negative self-talk, try this little tune! I call up my friends on the phone and sing into their recording devices. One friend keeps the songs and plays them to her friends. How delightfully embarrassing.

Here's my tune! I can hear the melody of "All day, all night, Marianne" sung by Harry Belafonte in that wonderful soft Caribbean style . . . mmmm.

Bliss in Bliss out, all day long
Bliss in Bliss out, I'm singing my song
Bliss in Bliss out, all day long,
Bliss in Bliss out, come, dance along.

Sounds, melodies and words are more than music to the ears – they vibrate with rhythms that inform the structure of our being. But that's another book! The important part to remember is that you have the power and ability to make a difference – in every thought you think, in your choices to create a life connected to beauty and truth, to more zest and joy in your life and those around you.

Reflections:
Do you have a favourite song that inspires you?
Do you remember an experience where you felt illuminated after a big challenge? How did it feel?
Are you connected with your Zest?

Are you ready to connect with your Zest?

Chapter 2

MAKE FRIENDS WITH YOUR SELF

"If you are not willing to risk the unusual,
You will have to settle for the ordinary.
Jim Rohn, Treasury of Quotes

TRUST. Five letters with a great meaning. It can keep the heart open in joy, or close it with suspicion. Do you trust yourself?

Would trusting your self be like discovering a pot of gold at the beginning and end of a rainbow? Ahhhh, how would you feel? Free? Jubilant? Singing and dancing like an Irish leprechaun? Well that pot of gold is found in the intelligence of your mind and the radiance of your heart. The relationship between your mind and your heart needs special attention, it must harmonize and align. That is true happiness and that is where you learn **trust.**

Our learning experiences here on earth are organized through relationships; family, friends, co-workers, the environment, our place in the cosmos. Yet the most important relationship you will ever have, the one which is the most precious gift of life, is the relationship you have with your Self. Really think on that. Most people give far more time to family members, friends, or are seduced by the ever glistening path of the "successful career". Yet, we are deeply emotional beings, and if we do not give time, space, or a compassionate ear within, we suffer. The hospitals are overflowing with the suffering. The worst is our isolation. The body and spirit demand to be nurtured or the result is painful crippled ways of ill health, stuck patterns, unhappy relationships and often a really bad attitude.

Many people are constantly in a state of physical or mental stress which is negative – and the spiritual/emotional needs which have largely been ignored, are now overwhelming issues in our society. Our minds are so overwhelmed with information overload – thank goodness we close our eyes at night to let the thoughts get sorted out! I know many people simply watch television to "numb out or unwind" at the end of the day, yet that can be very dangerous. What we really do is put in another load of information – most of which is designed by the media to manipulate our systems for impulse buying! We lose control of being able to balance the mind by continuously increasing the information and the mind begins fragmenting. Most of us want more control and power in our lives, so why are we giving up our control to the TV or Internet?

Have you ever listened to your mind take off with all of its thoughts? Hahahahaha is it ever funny. Meditation teachers just howl over the disconnected fragments of thoughts that people have running through their heads. It used to be called multi-tasking and some researchers are now showing that it is actually harmful. For example – I start out thinking about my aunts in Saskatchewan, then, how cold it is in the winter in Saskatchewan; winter specials for Mexico, a two mile long white beach I used to walk on in the Bahamas, a deadline for a presentation. Next the book Huckleberry Finn and finally what I was going to make for supper. What in the world do all those thoughts have to do with one another? People might call it association, I think it is fragmentation.

Our mind is the most exquisitely engineered, diligent, fascinating and incredible interactive piece of artwork ever created. It is designed to be working all the time, and it does. 24/7. It is like the most intricate watch with tiny wheels constantly going round all interconnecting with various other wheels. This is why you want to be very careful what information you are letting inform you and be part of your system. Visual stimulus is a powerful teacher and we accept images and visuals very quickly.

Thinking about our minds and how much they have to do, it is no wonder we feel overwhelmed, stressed or fragmented. It's like feeling disconnected from your heart, who you really are, the place where you are a friend to yourself.

When I ask people who is their best friend, they often say, Clare, Joe, my sister, my dog. Then I ask them who wakes up with you first thing every morning and goes to bed with you every night, no exceptions, is it your best friend Clare or Joe? They look very puzzled, like what are you talking about. If Clare and Joe are your best friends and they are not with you every minute of your day, perhaps you might want to also consider being your own best friend.

Think about it. You wake up every morning with you; you go to sleep every night with you. Clare and Joe are not there in your dreams, wrestling with the sheets or your life experiences. They do not live inside your skin, see through your eyes or eat your food. Even your dog, no matter how loving and perceptive it is, can not think your thoughts for you. Only you can and do.

Please use the lines after the questions to write anything down – remember this is your book to use, so scribble away.

Question: What is friendship to you? Jot down your ideas.

____

____

____

____

Then think about your best friend. Hmm, who is this person?
Why are they my best friend?

____

What is your relationship like?

____

____

What do you do together?

____

____

How do you hang out with one another?

____

____

Would you tell a lie to them? Yes or No? __________

Would you make a promise and break it? __________

Would you apologize if you did something wrong in your friendship?

____

____

Would you then correct yourself and renew your friendship?

____

____

Would you willingly listen to them?

____

____

____

Would you give them time and space to simply be? How?

____

____

Do you appreciate them? How?

____

____

Do you comfort them? How?

Do you applaud and celebrate their achievements? How?

Now – How do you treat yourself?
Please take some time with this question.

I'll say it again – How Do You treat Yourself?

Question for you: Are you a friend to your self? How?

Think about your best friend again. Compare that relationship with how you treat yourself.

Do you tell lies to yourself? Or half-truths, that sound like they could be true?

Do you make a promise and break it?

Do you then correct yourself and keep your promise?

Do you apologize to yourself if you do something wrong, like break your values and beliefs? How?

Do you willingly take the time to listen to yourself, fears and all? This is a big one.

____

____

____

Do you give yourself time and space to simply be?

____

____

Do you appreciate yourself? How?

____

____

Do you comfort yourself? How?

____

____

Do you applaud and celebrate your achievements? How?

____

____

Think about some times you have broken promises to yourself. OUCH! The most obvious times are New Year's resolutions. You set out with great drive, enthusiasm, focus; then the habits, unresolved patterns and lack of deep friendship and support simply dissolve your intention.

Personally, I do not make resolutions anymore.

Suggestion: Perhaps see your life as a long learning experience and that you are involved in a certain activity. For myself, I always want to do well, yet do things in a way that keeps me in balance. I set goals with realistic deadlines and diligently work on better habits to focus myself for positive results. I still have bad habits, yet I get my balance back a little quicker each time. Please see Chapter 7 - Manifesting Your Dreams, to help you develop a path for your goals, dreams and visions to become a success in your life.

When you make resolutions or promises to yourself and break them, it breeds a degree of suspicion and sabotage throughout all your experiences. You build the space inside of you where there is no trust. If you can not trust yourself, neither will anyone else.

Hint. Here is a simple action for re-building trust. Apologize and forgive yourself. Notice what happens when you bend your head, place your hands on your heart and say, "I'm so sorry, please forgive me". Just notice the response your body gives.

Question: How do you make friends with your mind and heart? Any ideas?

If you are willing to agree that you have an innate consciousness or intelligence inside of you that is responding, and running your body, why not see what happens if you say hello to your inner self? Like this: "Hello to the beautiful mind in my body! Thank you for every gift you have given me. Thank you for doing every single thing I have asked you to do." Then wait and feel what the response is. What do you notice?

Say something compassionate to your heart, and feel that response. "Beloved heart, thank you for carrying all my emotional burdens, for healing the wounds, for the courage to walk forward in life. Thank you for all the love and compassion." Notice the response.

Treating your self like an intelligent, gifted, resourceful and unique expression of creativity would be a great place to make a friendship pact. Friendship is based on trust, especially trust within.

Here's an interesting new place to check out. There is a research centre called the Heart Math Institute (www.heartmath.org). Some of their research indicates that there are brain cells within the heart. My chiropractor says the brain and spinal cord are the first to be developed in the human body. The Institute research indicates that it is not until the brain cells within the heart fire and the heart beats, that the brain and neural systems engage. Interesting. The heart's intelligence engages and then the brain is stimulated to function. To me that means there is a direct pathway of intelligence between the heart and mind, which also means there is the direct influence from the heart to the entire system of the body. What or who fires the brain cells in the heart? Is it love?

Mystical Sufi poet Hafiz observed, "I have estimated the influence of reason upon love and found that it is like that of a raindrop upon the ocean, which makes one little mark upon the water's face and disappears."

Reflections:

Have you listened to your heart lately? What do you hear?
Where is the spark of light inside of you?
What one thing would deepen your self relationship?
What could you do to be a better friend to yourself?

Who's in charge anyway?

Chapter 3

WHAT IS MEDITATION

"What you are speaks so loudly,
I can't hear what you say."
Ralph Waldo Emerson

Let's get right down to basics! Meditation is a process to de-clutter your mind and connect you within, to help your body stay healthy or bring it back to health. Meditation also builds awareness, focus, clarity, creativity, intelligence, communication and courage. Just face some fears and see how quickly your courage starts to build!

Think about our everyday lives – what we do to stay healthy. We take out the garbage, wash the dishes, brush our teeth and have a shower, clean off the old makeup, and shave. We clean things up on a regular basis to freshen up our homes, eat well, clean our bodies, and present ourselves to the world, to participate in life's adventure in a healthy way.

Now what would happen with your health, if you continued to eat off your dirty dishes every day? Let's say you ate every meal off one dish and left it unwashed for a week. Imagine little bits of Monday's hardened gooey egg mess and meat loaf, Tuesday's broccoli bits with soy scrapings, Wednesday's macaroni and cheese dinner with some chocolate syrup from dessert, Thursday's lasagna, Friday's fish with white sauce, perhaps a bit of mold, and a few sneezes. All on one plate. And you look at it every time you put fresh food on it. Yummmy!

If you kept eating off that plate week in and week out, how long before the poison of that old decaying food would make you ill?

Would your food be appetizing or disgust you?

____

Would you be disgusted with yourself?

____

Would you invite people over to share a meal with you and serve them off your dirty plate?

____

Meditation is like washing the dirty dishes of our thoughts, or taking out our mental garbage so we do not smell or look like a dirty unwashed plate. That's pretty clear, eh?!

You have somewhere between 10,000 to 60,000 thoughts per day! Researchers say that of those thoughts, about 80% are negative. So, how or when do you wash out the negative thoughts? Consider all those negative thoughts like garbage. Meditation is taking out the garbage, so your mind can be clear, focused, present and your body working at optimum efficiency. It is the shortcut to clearing out the clutter and going quickly to the ah-hah! moments, inspirational thoughts, and juice of life. What I love to call Zest.

When you take out the old garbage type thoughts you have space for light and joy to create new experiences and well being. Otherwise, you run on garbage and poison yourself to death – mentally, physically, emotionally and spiritually.

Meditation will grease the wheels of every single thing you want to accomplish in your life. It's the truth. That's why I developed the One Minute Active Meditation technique – it absolutely helped me and I know it can help you.

Meditation Myths - that's right, MYTHS!

The biggest myth of meditation is that it is passive. It never is. You might be sitting still, yet so much is going on, if you started to explore the wonder of who you are, it would amaze you.

Myth: Meditation is so hard to do.

Truth: If you choose an active process with visualizations, breathing, and freedom to move – it's easy.

Myth: Everyone has to sit still for an hour every day.

Truth: The way I am teaching you, after you build the basic foundation, you just tune in throughout your day and whenever you want, tune it up with a longer session.

Myth: It's too complicated!

Truth: People have made the concept of meditation complicated. There are thousands of meditations you can do, many with totally different benefits. All are meant to focus the mind and bring awareness within. It can be fun, easy and simple.

Myth: Meditation is some sort of weird religion.

Truth: Meditation is to clear the clutter so you can focus, be present and be more aware of yourself – creating space for creativity, clarity and mental intelligence. Is sitting still and listening a weird religion? Getting to know your self is a delightful and very funny process!

Myth: People fall asleep.

Truth: They actually go in to a deep resting state. The body has its' own intelligence and will make you rest if you are too tired or full of food.

Myth: You must have a teacher.

Truth: Having a teacher can make you feel more secure – they can also help you speed up your understanding. Yet, in the end you are the book of life and you came to explore your life. Learn to cherish making the time for finding out the amazing secret you.

Myth: I will do it wrong.

Truth: You can never have a bad meditation or do it wrong - impossible. Any time you give yourself and your mind permission to sort your thoughts out and connect within, amazing things happen. The trick here is to build your awareness with a good foundation then tune in throughout your day. All silence creates a deepening of intentional activity within. As you continue to listen within, you will feel more comfortable with yourself and that builds trust.

Let's explore some terms.

Passive Meditation.

In this process, you just allow all your thoughts to come up. Generally people are seated and quite still while in meditation. They observe the thoughts, let them dance around. That's it! It drives many people crazy as the freight trains of thought take off in the mind. Some people can hardly sit still. It can take a long time to achieve some inner calm and peace, especially for beginners. 10,000 to 60,000 thoughts every day – WOW.

People see this as a passive form of meditation, yet what is really going on is a world of information, intelligent communication and focus. This is a highly interactive process that involves your entire being in a very quiet manner. It took me a long time to be able to sit still and learn how to be with my thoughts. I still prefer actively working with them.

Active Meditation.

In this form of active meditation – you participate mentally, often physically, using different techniques. This could involve placing Intent, "I will do the One Minute Meditation every day for one month." You set a specific goal in your mind and do it. Some techniques are walking a labyrinth, a guided visualization, chanting or toning, specific breathing patterns, focusing on a candle flame, yoga, prayer, even ironing the laundry. The trick is to feel how the inner wisdom is working as you consciously engage your mind for harmonious alignment to intelligently communicate with your body as a living entity, not something you are dragging around. The benefits can magnify quickly.

Both types of meditation will create space within you, so you can focus on doing what you want to do and be how you want to be. The mind remembers everything, the body has memories stored in the tissues and in the bones. Movement, sound, listening in and placing intent help release the memories and clear the clutter. The goal is to be aligned, in harmony, full of zest or bliss.

When you really understand the beauty, truth and gift of connecting within, you might choose the longer passive style of sitting still, observing and listening. You can explore the deep inner world of meditation where you engage the universe within. As you are willing to engage, the magic of your being emerges. At some point in all forms of meditation, you realize that your personality is not in charge; it is simply a participant that affects the joy of the life experiences.

I have participated in meditation groups since 1987 and taught various forms of active meditation since 1998. My teachers have been yogis, enlightened masters, shamans, Buddhists, my own angels and guides, sound, breath, movement, visualizations and the years of practice with clients. The training of hypnotherapy was incredible in exploring and comparing modern techniques with the ancient practices of shamanism. Curiosity deepened my learning curve!

After many years of teaching and holding workshops, it boils down to this - people come for three major reasons:

- ✓ Physical health
- ✓ Mental health
- ✓ Spiritual health and healing

Most people know meditation can do these things:

- ✓ Lower blood pressure
- ✓ Decrease anxiety and stress
- ✓ Decrease acute and chronic pain
- ✓ Increase breathing capacity
- ✓ Improve concentration and focus
- ✓ Inspire a sense of peace and well being

People are slow to realize that meditation makes you more intelligent, creative and full of life. Meditation can open the doorway for tremendous insights, information, "ah-hah" moments, and provide all the details you need to design a project. It is a highly logical process.

I truly believe that all the people who come to my classes and workshops are really coming as spiritual seekers. In spiritually seeking they are healing, physically, mentally and emotionally. We have lots of fun trying out all kinds of ideas for meditations, building awareness, laughing with each other and sharing some of the greatest stories. Some people are so visual and have the wildest imaginative stories. Yet, their stories make perfect sense to them. It refers to their life and helps them understand situations.

Here are a few examples:
One person had cartoon characters that always came to her rescue as she faced her fears. Remember the tv show and

movie with Scooby Doo? Well, Scooby and the gang would always show up. Another person would get unzipped, peeled, layers removed as she worked through clearing some deep personal emotional issues. I could not have imagined how many ways there are of being peeled. Another person ended up in a Mad Hatter's tea party – the work stress situation in their life was intense. In some meditations with drumming, animals came and showed people through the forest, helped them fly, they discovered secret treasure groves. In the Angel meditations, it felt like the entire room wafted with grace and heavenly warmth. We also played with colors and Goddess cards and sacred geometry images. Anything that would trigger the body and the imagination to open up and explore new perceptions.

My own experiences have shown me herbs for healing, answers to questions, learning new ways to communicate and respect myself, as well as making me face my bad habits. I really enjoyed working with sound – drums, flutes, toning. With toning we would gather in a group and create harmony with a sound like Ohm. For 5 minutes we continued to make the one sound, then stopped and just let ourselves feel the vibrations. It felt like the room and all my cells were vibrating, as if the sound vibration was breathing through me. It is very healing and so enriching.

Sometimes when people asked me to interpret dreams or their meditation journeys, instead of telling them my perception, I asked them to go within and say "I do not get it, please tell me in a way I can understand". Interesting to note, the story changed immediately and they understood. A fascinating process.

So, I learned that this infinite intelligence literally will communicate with you in whatever way it thinks you can understand and will keep giving you that information until you either get it or you make it clear that you do not get it.

People have shared every type of story from their meditation experiences – deep personal healing from abuse, victim stories, archetype stories, dramas and perception shifts, joyous stories of celebration. Each and every time, the person would undergo a dramatic shift in their own being and ability to hold more light by simple showing up and participating in a meditation. Even if they said their mind was busy like a train barreling down the tracks with 10,000 thoughts, you could see the light of connection shine in their eyes. After all, it takes the mind a little bit of time to unclutter all those thoughts before it can be free to help you understand some new things.

Meditation is also important for the physical health of your body and understanding the energy field that emanates from within you and surrounds you. That vitality or zest from the heart of your being. I think that all the new advances in science and medicine just like Quantum physics, will be devoted to studying vibration, thought wave patterns and energy. Einstein in his later years said he was totally fascinated with studying light and the energy it produced.

So, remember the quote at the top of the page?

"What you are speaks so loudly, I can't hear what you say."

Everyone knows that funny sense of walking in to a room and feeling that you could cut the tension in the air with a knife. So what is that? Feelings about to explode? What are feelings but thought energy? We talk about undercurrents in conversations, intuition, gut feel, looking in some one's eyes and knowing they are lying. You can watch someone's body language when they speak and know what they say out their mouth is not what their body is communicating to you. They are not speaking the truth. Everyone knows these things, yet what is it?

That same intuition, feeling or sensing is so very apparent in animals. They are incredible teachers and are highly tuned in to energy. A friend said to me her family noticed their dog would be laying down ears twitching, enjoying puppy dreams, then suddenly get up and go wait by the door. They knew that she would be home within 15 minutes. The dog repeated this time after time with no way of knowing when she would be coming home, and she usually came home within the 15 minutes!

Remember the devastating Tsunamis in Indonesia, how the animals went to the higher grounds? Animals simply do not have all the clutter we carry around with us and therefore tune in to the vibrations and certain frequencies that enable them to know and interpret things many people still think or call mysterious.

We all have a "personal space or energy field" around our bodies. Most people feel uncomfortable when another person is within this personal space, unless they are a good friend or there is a sense or feeling of some form of enjoyment in the closeness. I feel that our personal space or energy field emanates from the very core of our being and vibrates with the thoughts we hold in our mind, body and soul. This field extends approximately 2 – 3 feet around our entire body. Now, that's quite a lot of information.

Hint:
Whenever you are within someone's field you may notice certain qualities or thoughts. I suggest you begin to know what are your thoughts and what belongs to someone else. Just notice. Some people have extremely strong energy fields and they can almost impose their mental strength upon you and leave you constantly thinking about them. This is a good indication that your personal boundaries and energy field needs some attention.

Your body is designed to work as a complete unit, whole and healthy, via a network of intelligent cells that actually heal and transform it via vibrations. When you are in a room with a number of people or even one other person, that field of energy transfers in thought waves or layers of vibration. You communicate in spoken and unspoken ways and patterns. That's how tarot readers and psychics read your cards and get a high rate of accuracy – they are sensitive enough to feel and interpret your body thought energy as well as see how your thought energy has chosen the cards. This is also how medical intuitives' can get such clear pictures of what dis-ease process is affecting you and the mental thoughts that might be associated with it. In Regression therapy or Hypnotherapy, you can actually see and feel a person respond as their body and systems remembers living through a childhood or past life trauma.

For you Guys, your body language reveals your deepest thoughts - this is how women know what you are thinking! Watch out!

A short story.

In 1997, I participated in a year long part-time training in Hypnotherapy. Every Monday night was a new adventure learning about energy, the mind, past-life regressions, out-of-body experiences, soul memories, angels, presence of spirit, and modern psychology. My teacher was a person who would explore anything, challenge the status quo and usually had a devilish twinkle in her eyes.

In one class we explored the ideas of a "moral code in the DNA". Was it possible that at some level in a person's true core, there was an intrinsic knowledge of what was right and wrong?

I remember the story our teacher shared with us; one fairly well known psychiatrist who also worked with hypnotherapy was curious about the same question. Was there in fact something like "intrinsic morals" built in to our systems? He set up a simple experiment. He brought in some women who were prostitutes, said he would pay them, and asked them to take off their clothes. None of the women had a problem and they began taking off their clothes. When they were nude, he asked them if they had any qualms about being nude in front of him. They laughed and slyly said, "No Doc, what else can we do you?" He then asked them to put their clothes back on.

The next step was to have them sit down and using Hypnotherapy, talk them in to a deep meditative or trance state. He was curious to find out, when a person's personality issues and defenses were quieted, what would their true nature reveal? What might be the response?

At the point when each woman was in a deep trance state, he gave the same instruction. Please take off your clothes. None of the women would do it. One woman blushed.

Interesting. Certainly not a double blind experiment in a laboratory. Yet, it opens the doorway to wondering what is in the heart or intrinsic core of our being that so defines our experience and leads us on our path. Is there an inherent code of truth within us? Hypnotherapy or Regression therapy by a trained person, is a highly valuable tool, yet self hypnosis or deep meditation can also provide many of the same benefits.

The energy dynamic created through the learned traits of the personality can often lead a person deeply astray of their true nature. In meditation we can learn to re-align ourselves with our true nature, beauty and live as the Yogis would say "in Bliss" or full of Zest which is at the depth of our creative being.

In this amazing field of energy work and spirituality – however you like to define it - the quality of meditating and listening takes on a new form as you learn to interpret the vibrations and field of energy that emanates from and surrounds yourself and other people. Your thoughts and the knowledge within you really do create your world.

Reflections:

How many negative thoughts a day do you have?
What do you hear when you listen to yourself?
What do you feel or hear when you are in a person's energy field?
How could meditation benefit you?
What is your current emotional challenge?
When could you make time in one minute segments to meditate?

How about taking out your mental garbage, so you can feast on your life?

Chapter 4

SPIRITUAL PUSHUPS

"Every beginning is a consequence.
Every beginning ends something."
Paul Valery, French Poet

. . .And ONE and TWO and THREE. If your body is a mirror of your inner world, how are those glutes, thighs, and abs? Time for a little assessment? I'm joking, yet really, our body does reflect our attitudes in life. Spiritual pushups are about defining and developing our personal emotional and spiritual strength through all of life's challenges. Let's assess your values, compassion, forgiveness and especially self-care. In what shape are the philosophies, religious traditions, guidelines or systems that guide your life? This is where meditation can really help you.

____

____

____

____

____

These are challenging questions and worth the time to reflect on. Truly, this is your one wild and precious life – what is the little engine which is keeping your heart pumping and alive with zest?

- Faith? _______
- Hope? _______
- Illusion? ______

- Love? ________
- Money? _______
- Career importance? _______
- Other? _________

I know many people feel overwhelmed and often frustrated, (there are so many concerns in our lives and the world) yet, as soon as your inner world comes back into alignment, then your body and outer world have good opportunities to do the same. As you see how the challenging experiences are shaping you to make you stronger, you can stand taller, let your heart be free and feel more alive.

Back to spiritual pushups . . . And ONE and TWO and THREE.

A short story.

The last time I went through the spiritual pushup routine was a four-year journey. Big challenges. I was so busy creating stuff and work and helping people around me, it felt like a marathon race had replaced bliss and joy, and that zest for my life had gone. I was on the treadmill of work and responsibility. Here's my tale.

My husband and I separated and agreed to divorce. Difficult and painful beyond words. The grace and ease was that we helped one another with our parting. Our thirteen-year life journey together had been filled with amazing adventures. For over 3 years, we sailed from San Francisco through the Panama Canal and around the Caribbean. We shared near-death experiences, awe-inspiring wonder and finally leaving the boat to take up the landlubber life again. It is said people come together for a reason, a season, or a lifetime. We suffered the classic tale of growing apart - our reason for being together was over. We wanted very different things. The pain, bewilderment, feelings of loss were worse than anything I had ever imagined it could be. It was the beginning of a deep transition to a new life.

Soon after my husband and I parted, my 85-year-old mother became ill. When a person divorces, the whole family goes through the transition. My mother and I are very close; emotional energy surges between us. We call it our ESP connection. I started running – literally, doctors, hospitals, naturopaths, and herbalists. We talked about our emotions and healing, prayed, worked with color therapy, changed diets, did cleanses, got massages. At one point, her health stabilized and then suddenly, just as I signed the papers to divorce, a huge lymphoma (cancer) appeared. If I hadn't learned lessons of compassion and letting go from all of this – I was back doing pushups . . .and ONE and TWO, and THREE. I had some arm strength now!

Somewhere in that same time, I moved and tried to sell or give away nearly all the physical possessions from my marriage years. When you let go, really let go! Only when I had the space inside, could I fill it with a new life. I took a course from the local church called "Divorce Care" and learned that it often takes people one year to heal the emotional, spiritual energy, for every four years you are together. We had thirteen years together, hmm, lots of work. I set the intent to clear myself of all the old wounds and stories and to treasure all the gifts. It takes time and persistence and the **willingness** to engage yourself in the healing process. I noticed with my clients that time alone did not heal anything – the scars were obvious in their everyday lives and habits.

Then, I just gave it all to the Infinite Intelligence within. I surrendered and asked to be taken care of – it was all I could do and the smartest thing I have ever done. Why? Because the sense of peace and support was amazing. My mother became the number one priority. My value system is this: conscious work with the Infinite Intelligence, then family, then career. Somewhere in all the fears and hospital visits and doctors' advice, I dealt with all my family responsibilities, yet did not have the time or space to do my deeper personal work. It was like a black pot of soup simmering away on the back burner. I knew my time would come. Through it all, I kept letting go and worked diligently with several techniques just to keep my balance. I finally brought all the techniques together in to the process I am going to teach you in this book – the One Minute Active Meditation Technique. I am endlessly grateful to my friends who supported me through all these very difficult times. Yet, the deepest friendship I began to understand and develop was my friendship within, my friendship with my self. A new best friend – me. When I noticed the negative thinking or beating myself up, and observing how much pain, time, effort and energy went in to all those thoughts - it was a real motivator to change.

Finally it became my time and I had the space to clear the deep clutter. People fall apart or keep dragging the same old woundology around because they never find a way, or willingly grieve and let go, over significant loss.

"He that lacks time to mourn,
lacks time to mend."
William Shakespeare

One spiritual pushup after another, we both came through. It was a long, persistent challenging journey. At the time I write this, my mother is close to her 90th birthday. Aging requires great strength. She has enough spark to flirt and cause a little trouble. Whoo Hoo! I am on to my next change and transition with joy and light inside and surrounding me. When you clear the clutter and have space inside, make sure you fill up with and align to truth and beauty, you will glow!

What a journey! What a teacher my mother is. How blessed I am. I believe we are here on planet earth to learn lessons and have experiences. One thing that stands out is how painful those lessons can be, especially if the experience has not taught you what you need to learn and the lesson gets repeated. Over, and over, and over again.

So, no matter what your life has been like until now – you may have gone through some big spiritual pushups – if not, I can guarantee you that at some point, you too will know the depth of that emotional work. It does make you stronger to withstand life's challenges. It can show you where you are missing the path and take you to greater compassion or forgiveness. It also clears the space of some deep clutter that you could use for a lot more fun in life. Zest anyone?

Some spiritual pushup areas:

- Low self-esteem
- Childhood abuse
- Grieving
- Divorce
- Letting go
- Death
- You're own severe illness
- Earthquakes
- Tsunamis
- Invasion of your country
- Endless work place strife
- Transitions in your life not fully grieved and released

What does your list look like?

____

Let's take another look at those glutes and thighs and abs? How about those underarms: do you have angel wing triceps flapping around? The shape your body is in, the lines on your face, the suppleness of your back, the glow in your eyes, they all relate to that inner friendship, the place where you let of the old stuff and connect with the spirit within. The harmony of your alignment with truth, values, beliefs, and attitudes – the place where your zest, creativity, and connection to the light within can shine. Now that's a good reason to make friends with you, listen in, make choices of joy and not negativity. Meditation will help you create just that!

Reflections:
What spiritual pushups have you done?
When did you choose the truth? How did it feel?
Have you smiled at yourself in the mirror lately?

Will you unleash your spirit and let it shine?

Chapter 5

INFINITE INTELLIGENCE

"To exist is to change,
to change is to mature,
to mature is to go on
creating oneself endlessly."
Henri Bergson, French philosopher

Changing bad habits and facing challenges is an interesting task, n'est-ce pas? I found those spiritual pushups got easier and easier as I harmonized with the Infinite Intelligence within.

Question: What the heck are you talking about, Infinite Intelligence within?

Okay. To start exploring this question let's look at the human body. Most people have not studied anatomy and physiology, at least not the internal workings of the human body! Yet somewhere in all of the complex highly interactive structure of the body there is a place where there is a living spark of energy holding the life force, patterns and intelligence of the human being. Look around you at everything in nature – perfect structure, a tree is a tree, a daffodil is a daffodil, a rabbit is a rabbit, not a big mouse. Certainly no one can tell you **exactly** what is this spark of energy within us that forms us, keeps us alive, keeps us breathing and takes over fully as soon as we sleep.
Do you know?

We like to give names to things, like the autonomic nervous system, the circulatory system, the lymphatic system. Well, who is in charge of that? How come it knows exactly what to do? How is it that all of these systems work together in one exquisitely designed unit? How in the world did we start out as an egg and a sperm that can only be seen under a microscope and turn out in to these amazing creations?

We just walk around in this human body enveloped in a skin, and talk about it as if we really know what is going on and we give things names. This does that because that's the way it is supposed to do things. We pretend to "discover" something that has always been there. As the saying goes, most of us know a lot more about our cars that we do the inner workings of our bodies! Very funny. Let's keep exploring.

On another level, let's say the existential, religious or philosophic planes, people believe or attempt to understand what we are doing here. Grand theories abound. We have been gifted by God to come and have a learning experience. It is our Karma, we will be re-incarnating until we get it right. We are a drop in the ocean participating in some cyclic pre-ordained plan. We come from different planets, that is why we have different races. We are the chosen ones. The earth was created through the weaving of Spider woman's web of creation. Some people just accept the fact that we are born, live and die. That's it. I think we are here to learn to love, as deeply, compassionately as possible, until we shine like a beautiful pearl.

Which story do you believe? How does that shape your life?

____

____

____

____

____

Well, what a curious lot we all are. Curiosity is an essential trait of learning, having a full life and getting into just a little bit of trouble. We certainly seem to enjoy our learning curves and all our “stories” have certainly caused more than a bit of trouble.

A short story.

I was always curious, very sensitive and felt different. I did not feel that I fit in very well. In every family the growing up years are challenging. My parents certainly presented us with their themes and challenges. We went through all the usual family dramas, illnesses and issues. Children are highly sensitive to energy and the currents of emotions – often responding to something that they can not put in to words. In an ideal world communication would be easy.

Reflecting now on my childhood experiences, the best things that I learned were that laughter, playing, dancing, singing and prayer were like good food, maintaining the body and health. When sickness occurred, my parents went to colour therapy, nutrition, the infamous Master Cleanse-lemonade diet (thank goodness without cayenne pepper which really burns going out the other end), breathing exercises, acupuncture, and studying where one was out of balance. The last resort was medical intervention with antibiotics or surgery.

They studied all the information that was available and worked on their inner process and connection. There was a knowingness of the body’s ability to heal, the innate wisdom or consciousness of life force within, and that it responded. They were, in my opinion, way ahead of their time. In the 1950’s, they explored the Kabalarian Society, which consisted of numerology east meets west, yoga philosophy. They combined that with good old hellfire and damnation Baptist religion. It was quite the mix of spiritual teachings and energy. My parents both changed their names according to numerology and gave my two siblings and me names to balance with the family name. Now, how crazy was that in the 1950's?

Back to curiosity - what a great trait! I deeply wanted to understand this innate intelligence and what was going on inside of me. The growing up years had left some big questions. Who am I? What was my purpose in life? I was curious and terrified. My studies and life took me along all the themes, hopes and challenges of my parents and then I delved into other aspects of holistic health. I was searching outside of myself for years trying to understand with my head, at the same time being told by various spiritual and psychic intuitives, that I was deeply intuitive.

The training as a Registered Massage Therapist gave me a tremendous understanding of what the inside of the body looked like. What a design! Deeper philosophic answers came through hypnotherapy and teachings in the shamanic traditions. I remember when I first read an article about Shamanism in the local Shared Vision magazine. My body went through a massive kinesthetic response - like being on fire. It was all I could do to stay seated and keep reading. It was if my entire being said "You found it!" I paid attention.

Later came essence work of understanding vibrations and sound, what power is and how you hold it cleanly, with joy and an open heart. Then my clients, bless their hearts, gave me the endless gifts of practice, and more practice and every experience became a teacher. Wow, what a journey of deepening into the mystery of whom we are.

So, that's part of my journey, now let's get back to you and more of this body understanding to get you closer to this Infinite Intelligence within.

Let me ask you some questions. How do you run your liver? Do you know how many functions it has? Depending on whom you talk to, it performs over three hundred functions. Do you get up every morning and say "Okay Liver, today you are going to break down all those phyllo pastries I had last night, get the hormone level back up for my thyroid, increase the bile to the gall bladder, take up glucose, minerals, and vitamins from portal and systemic blood and store them!! Oh sure you do. Ridiculous, right?

Okay, what about your heart? Do you get up every morning and tell your heart exactly how many beats per minute you want it to do, no skipping, no racing, and clear the cholesterol, oxygenate the lungs, spend a little extra time getting the blood to your feet because they are always cold? How about telling the AV node to steady the electrical current so that if you have a sudden scare, you will not have a heart attack? Kidneys? Intestines? How about telling your body how to break down, digest and process all the food you eat? Have you ever seen the inside of your intestines? More ridiculousness!

You leave every vital process in your body to the innate consciousness or Infinite Intelligence that created you and holds the patterns of health that run every function in your body as a whole unit. That is the Infinite Intelligence within you, the creative spark and intuitive voice that is really running your body.

You have the infinite pleasure of running around in a Rolls Royce or Mercedes type vehicle. Your choice is whether to create a crash and burn dumpster derelict (with all your learning curves, nasty experiences, bad habits and that quite amazing complex personality filled with attitude) or polish and refine both the outer and inner self to reflect the light of the shimmering beauty of this Infinite intelligence from within. I call it the co-creative journey of your soul, spirit and body, a place of Zest.

Here's a hint! What if you talk with the Infinite Intelligence within you – that enlivening life spirit that forms the essence of your being. Guess what might happen? Is it possible you might remember your inner spirit friend, a knowingness that you have forgotten since childhood?

What I am saying is that you can connect to the Infinite Intelligence within you. You can experience it as alive, wondrous and fully participating with you in co-creating your life. Live as one being: your soul, your spirit, your mind, and your heart.

Ask, Seek, Knock
"Ask and it will be given you,
seek and you shall find,
knock, and the door will be opened to you.
For everyone who asks, receives; he who seeks, finds;
and to him who knocks, the door will be opened."
Matthew 7.7 Christian Bible

Sounds just like placing intent for
conscious connection within.

Would you agree?

I devised the One Minute Active Meditation for anytime, anywhere – in a meeting at work, driving the car, at the supermarket, walking down the street and so forth, to help you organize your mind, calm and connect within, remember details, and understand difficult issues or challenges. The Infinite Intelligence within you is always working to keep you in balance and loving. That is the natural state. It knows how to take out the mental trash and bring synchronicity, how to connect you with your intuition, creativity, health, wisdom and Zest for life. Remember that it's an inside job!

Reflections:
What does Infinite Intelligence mean to you?
What are you curious about in your life experiences?
Where does the spark of life reside in you?

Curious?

Chapter 6

BUILDING THE FOUNDATION

"Great minds have purposes,
Others have wishes."
Washington Irving, American Essayist

In this chapter, we are going to go through what to do, and why it is important! Everything needs a good foundation in life and meditation needs that too.

The purpose of this chapter is to go through all the explanations for building a good foundation for the One Minute Active meditation. Remember, once you have the foundation built, it never leaves, or is destroyed – doing the guided meditation several times will help you anchor in the ideas and feelings of connections. Then you can connect easily and quickly in one minute segments and receive the benefits. So, pick up the book, and go through the fun visualization. People tell me that playing the guided meditation on the CD works the best, you choose. Tune in and tune up. As you strengthen your inner connection, you will feel that Infinite Intelligence and that place of zest or life spirit expand.

Please read through all the ideas in the chapter once or twice so you really understand what you are doing, then do the 30 minute guided meditation with the CD to build your foundation.

Make a date with yourself!

Call it My Date with Destiny, or Making Friends with Me or Finding Me! You'll need about 30 minutes. You've got a nifty project to accomplish – and the project is making a deeper connection between your head and your heart and your innate wisdom and infinite intelligence. You are building your foundation for meditation. Let's go!

- Choose a quiet safe space that is well ventilated.
- Choose a comfy chair that supports your head.
- Feet flat on the floor and perhaps get a warm blanket.
- Turn off the telephones, televisions, computers, and all gadgets.

(Noise will magnify, so inform the family or significant others, this is a "Do Not Disturb" time. Or get out of the house and go to a quiet space; even your workplace could be good if you have a private office or room. Keep your date with yourself and make it special. You are worth it.)

Sit in the comfy chair and close your eyes. You will stay seated in the chair for 30 minutes. That's the agreement with your self. Do not get up. That's part of the date! Remember all the instructions are to build a foundation for meditation.

Now notice when you close your eyes, how your senses start tingling. You have 350 plus sensory receptors. When you close your eyes they immediately compensate by increasing information to your brain. The old reptilian and limbic systems engage. Since we rely so heavily on our eyes for input, when the eyes are closed – BAM the systems go into overdrive trying to compensate.

This is really important. One of the reasons people jump out of the chair and end up across the room is the fear mechanism. Remember that fear is a four-letter word that means information. (Every emotion is connected with a story which is filled with information.) When you close your eyes, your ingrained training and personality say "Danger,

Danger, we can't see, we could be ATTACKED!" The fight or flight response snaps into gear and you burn rubber getting out of there. Whew. Saved. There are other reasons why we become so uncomfortable sitting still and closing our eyes. Many people have trained themselves to constantly multi-task – just ask a mother of small children. The mind is running the program of Do-Do-Do-Do, often creating a jerky response as it continuously fires through the nerves. Whatever is going on, it is simply information telling you a story.

Soooo, you need to inform your brain in advance of the purpose and objective of your date! You are going to sit down, you will be closing your eyes and you want to connect with your heart. You want to connect with this infinite intelligence within, make friends with yourself and stay seated for 30 minutes. Heavens, you sit longer at a boring meeting. Please remember that this date is about you making friends with you.

Okay, back to your senses! Notice what you feel inside of you. Heart beating, breath in upper middle or lower chest, stomach gurgling, twitches, itchy nose; brain/mind trying desperately to engage in multi-tasking 2,000 thoughts. Simply notice.

Now, close your inner invisible eyelid. What's that? Well, camels have 3 eyelids to protect them from blowing sand. Birds and some reptiles also have 3 eyelids. When you close your eyelids you will notice you are still very sensitive to light. Closing those inner invisible eyelids shuts out more of the outside world and moves you deeper into your inner world. Think of a wall or screen coming down on the inside of your eyelids. Feel how your eyes suddenly seem heavy. Notice what happens. A sigh? Head feels a little heavy? Heart beat slowing down? Shoulders relax just a bit? Thoughts slowing down?

Important! Closing your inner eyelids tells your 350 plus sensory receptors to pay more attention to what goes on inside of you and sense your energy field around you! This opens the door to the magical space of self-healing, increased intuition, finding purpose and passion in life, aligning with the innate consciousness, tuning in with the place of zest and bliss within! Remember: keep those eyelids closed and stay in your seat.

At this point your brain might feel like it wants to explode. AAAAAAaaaahh all those thoughts. It's like a freight train barreling down the tracks. Remember, we have anywhere from 10,000 to 60,000 thoughts per day, most of them negative. So, depending on how fragmented your mind is or how many thoughts have not been organized in the mind . . . it's like the busiest store in a shopping mall at Christmas time! Let's give it some instructions to calm down!

Instruct your brain/mind to organize all the thoughts. Give it complete permission to synthesize, trash, retrieve, file and create order - do anything it needs to do to get balance with the 10,000 plus thoughts. Say something like this: "Please, Infinite Intelligence within me, unclutter my mind. Put all this information in the right categories and places, neat and tidy. Organize all the numbers, names, dates and thoughts, so I can retrieve them whenever I need or want to, easily and effortlessly. I'll give you 5 minutes. At the end of those 5 minutes, I would like it completed and my mind calm so it can prepare to do other work. Thank you. Begin now." Think of your brain as a computer. You have all this data and now you are going to click on Save. Asking/instructing your mind to organize all the data is the Save key.

How can the brain/mind do all that in 5 minutes? Think of the fastest computer ever created – now compare that to the speed of light. Your mind uses light energy, the frequency, colors, pitch, essence and vitality of light. Five minutes. If you really want to practice – get a timer and play with instructing your mind to clear the clutter in 5 minutes and time it. Have some fun.

When I have had a very busy day, and I ask my mind to organize all the thoughts, it hums, like a hive of busy bees. Yet, if I ask or instruct my mind to clear the clutter frequently throughout my day, once it knows exactly what I want done, the next time I place intent, it only takes a minute to clear the clutter.

Good, now let's spend a few minutes with the breath. In through your nose, out through your nose. Just like you've always done! Focus on breathing deep into your belly, pumping it up like a basketball. Hold the breath for a few seconds, then exhale. We breathe mostly in our upper chest and deprive the rest of our body of oxygen. The breath is your life force. Singers breathe deep into their bellies and backs. Our physical lungs occupy the space from the first rib to just below the rib cage, front and back. In yoga, the essential teaching is to learn to fill the entire lung space with the breath. Play with it.

If it helps, use the count of 6. Breathe in for 6 counts, hold the breath for 6 counts and exhale for 6 counts. When you regulate the breath, it also helps to calm and balance the mind and systems.

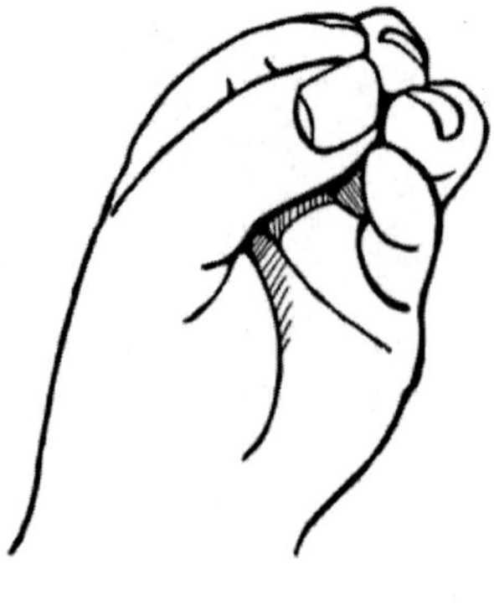

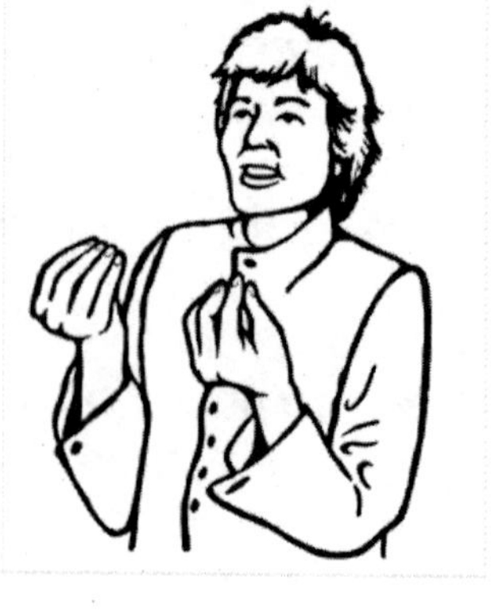

Now, while your mind is busy organizing all those thoughts, please put all the fingertips on one hand together and all the fingertips on the other hand together. According to Chinese Medicine and Reflexology, meridians or energy lines in your palms and every fingertip connect you with a certain part of the body's systems. In yoga, hand Mudras (specific combinations of finger positions) are like yoga for the body. In NLP (Neuro Linguistic Programming) you learn to anchor in feelings and sensations. You have a heightened positive experience and want to connect with a physical reminder, so you touch an area, like your hand, while feeling the emotion. Putting your fingertips together is your anchor to this meditation experience.

Brain research on people with strokes indicates that by pulsing the fingertips together on each hand stimulated both the right and left sides of the brain. I have found that connecting or applying a pressure stimulus to all the fingertips engages my brain and works to energize the systems in my body and energy field. We have all seen people pondering a situation with their fingertips pressed together like a pyramid, our body instinctively does something to help us achieve that quieter reflective awareness. Put your fingertips together, keep your hands apart, then touch all the fingertips together, sense and feel. What works best for you?

Some people experience a tingling sensation in their hands going up their arms, a warmth that spreads. Just hang out and breathe deeply. For the rest of the meditation, keep your fingertips on each hand together and your eyelids (especially those invisible eyelids) closed.

Great, now your mind has "Saved" all those loose bits of information, your fingertips are pulsing with energy and gently sending sensations up your arms, shoulders, and through your chest.

Here's the juicy bit that I always love to do: Visualize greeting the morning sun rising over the ocean. This visualization connects you with an immense presence, the spark of light inside of you. This is essential for anyone who has lost their meaning, purpose, passion, or zest for life. The Egyptians, Toltecs, Aztecs, Hopi and other indigenous peoples understood the sun as a physical extension of the eternal presence of life force. When I took tours to sacred sites in Sedona, Arizona and in the Hopi Nations, I discovered that the Hopi people who live high atop the mesas continue to sing the greeting of the Sun. They watch and pray as the sun rises over the horizon, receiving the first shafts of light into their eyes and mind, illuminating their journey of the day. They sing a song to greet the sun and then at the end of the day, they sing the song as the sun sets.

Their beautiful song goes something like this:

> Kuatay laynoh laynoh mau ah tay
> Hi yah noh, hi yah noh, hi yah noh.

The literal translation is:

> We are one, with the infinite Sun
> Forever and ever and ever.

Colour therapy in holistic health teaches us that receiving different shades of light onto our bodies is healing. White light holds the full spectrum of colour. If you shine light directly at the forehead it can stimulate the pineal gland – which influences our hormonal system as well as our inner vision. Just as people who suffer with SAD (Seasonal Affective Disorder) know very well, light is indispensable to their emotional stability in the wintertime.

(Caution: There is an eye healing technique with eye exercises to look directly at the Sun. I am NOT recommending this. It can harm the eyes.)

Remember in an earlier chapter I asked . . . "Have you ever greeted the morning sun and really watched what happens? The light filaments are colored, shimmering in the atmosphere. There is a tremendous sense of awakening in the mind. The sky is filled with an exquisite artistic display of warmth and illumination." When you learn to work and feel the vibrations of light, it actually feels like your being comes alive, sparkling, zinging with energy. The spark of light or Infinite intelligence within you is completely nourished by this light – whether you visualize it or let the sun's rays warm your skin. More Zest!

Ask your mind to fully participate in this visualization. "Please focus all my attention on creating this visualization of the rising sun on the ocean." Remember we are still going through all the understanding for building the foundation for meditation. This next part is best with the CD.

Visualize that you are seated on your favorite lounging chair on a warm white sandy beach. The beach stretches for miles in either direction. This is the tropical hideaway of your dreams. Feel the white silky smooth sand slide between your toes as you scrunch them. See the glistening aqua blue waters and hear the waves gently lapping on the shore. The palm trees with their fronds are ever so gently waving in the wind. The ocean is calm, so peaceful, and so tranquil. There is not a soul in sight, nothing and no one here at this moment to disturb your peace. On this special day, your date with destiny, you are here to begin a glorious new beginning in your life. The rising sun will help you illuminate your mind and soul with its eternal brilliance. It will connect you to the inner core of your being.

Notice the softness in the sky, a few puffy clouds tinged with pink streaks as you gaze over the ocean to the point where the sun will rise. See the heavens warming with the light, feel yourself anticipating the first glimpse, the rays of the sun's energy bursting upon you. Feel it, see it, and know it. As the rays begin shimmering on the water, rainbows of light stream straight to you, into your eyes, into your mind, into your heart and soul, waking you up and connecting you with the eternal flame of passion, purpose, meaning, joy and zest. These rays of light are the essence of your being. Fill up with it, enjoy, and breathe in life.

The sun is now halfway revealed. Majestic, immense, focused, in perfect alignment. You stand in awe, breathing deeply, engaged with the primal knowledge of light and life force. The heat warms every cell in your body. Life all around you is humming. Ask that you know yourself, that truth and wisdom are revealed in you. Ask that healing energy expand within you. Watch the sun transcend the waters. Feel the change in you. Notice everything that happens. Enjoy.

Then gently bring yourself back from this wonderful paradise and into your chair, in your very safe space. Eyes closed! Remember all the sensations. Feel your connection with the images and how the light affected you.

The final step, with your eyes and invisible eyelids closed, all your fingertips on each hand pressed together, your body illuminated in the warmth and light of the sun: Ask the Infinite Intelligence to expand within you so that you may know it in every cell of your being. As the Christian Bible says, "Ask and you shall receive"! Connect. Stay with that feeling for the next few minutes.

Great work! You have set the structural foundation for this meditation technique. Use the CD as often as you want to get the added benefits of the singing bowl with my voice and strengthen the foundation, or simply do the process using the directions.

Now that you have built the foundation for the One Minute Active Meditation you simply do these 4 steps anytime, anywhere and receive the instant benefits in just One Minute!

The One Minute Active Meditation Technique is:

1) Put your fingertips together.

2) Close your eyes (if it is safe to do so).

3) Take several deep breaths.

4) Ask or place intent for the Infinite Intelligence within you to expand and do whatever is needed in one minute.

By putting your fingertips together, breathing and placing intent, you are connecting to your own energy systems and the guided meditation with all the good feelings generated in the meditation. If you give your inner wisdom a time frame of one minute to accomplish a task, your inner wisdom knows to do it quickly. It is very helpful if you can be quiet when you make the request as this does take energy. Doing deep breathing will be fuel for the body and systems to go to work.

Now throughout your day – in meetings, walking along the street, caught in traffic (parking lot on the freeway), in a conflict, at night before bed, especially at night before bed - put all your fingertips together and ask the infinite intelligence to expand within you, dissolve the mental energy clutter, align, energize and center you. It will know exactly what to do, and your relationship with yourself will take on a whole new meaning.

I suggest you repeat the foundation steps several times to thoroughly anchor in the information and build this beautiful new place within. The more times you connect and clear the clutter, the easier life and living become.

Reflections:
What happens when you close your eyes?
What do you feel when you touch your finger tips together?
What does it feel like when your mind starts to calm down?

Are you ready to begin?

Chapter 7

MANIFESTING YOUR DREAMS

"Our plans miscarry because they have no aim.
When a man does not know what harbor
he is making for, no wind is the right wind."
Seneca the Younger, Roman statesman

It is all about you! And that's a good thing!

Here we are! The reason you bought the book, read my stories, and are doing the One Minute Active Meditations - you want more calm, less stress, increased energy, essentially a better perhaps a more simple life with zest, juice and passion! You want personal power and control over your choices in life. When your life is good and you are happy inside, that radiates like the energy of the sun. It is a magnet for more good things to happen. Zest, connection, creating good things in life.

A very short story.

A while back, I was in a men's clothing store looking for a gift. A fellow had stopped by the store to say hi to the owner. They were chit chatting about the changes in his life and the owner asked him, "So what do you think is the secret for a happy relationship?"

He replied, "Get your life how you want it to be. Have the job or career you want, the lifestyle, know yourself, then invite someone in."

She looked at him thoughtfully and he said "It was the most important thing I have ever done in my life and I am happy."

Good advice.

Sometimes people have looked at me in a bewildered sort of way, saying, "I don't know what I want. If I can't figure out what I want, I'm still lost." I suggest you work with this One Minute Active Meditation technique and the Infinite Intelligence within to find out. To help yourself on your journey of knowing what you want, ask yourself the following three questions until every bone in your body is satisfied with the answers. Let them roll around in your mind, be dreamy, give your self permission to have something new or simply be in a new way. Start with yourself, do you want some personal changes? Think about communication in your family – that should provide some desire for changes!

1) What do I want in life? (Think BIG in every aspect of your current life. Be very specific.) Family, health, relationships, career, travel, finances etc.

2) What will it look like? Do this for each area.

____
____
____
____
____
____
____
____

3) Who is there with me?

____
____
____
____

Keep asking yourself these three questions until you are crystal clear, then write down all the details to design your future. Put pictures on a collage or vision board, knowing that, at this moment in time, this what you want to do and where you want to go. Have fun. Be outrageous. Laugh and dream – give yourself permission to have anything. **Then come back to the place of what is really right for you.** We can all dream BIG, yet knowing what really is right for you – that is joy. You will know what is right for you when your body just relaxes with the images and feelings. It just feels right.

So, make several boards and hang one in the kitchen, one in the bathroom, one in the bedroom and one at work. Keep your eyes focused on what you want. Know what the end point is of your goal. Have clear parameters of what it will look like. Be curious. Listen, Listen, and Listen. Know your internal voice, your intuition. Ask questions like what if and why not? Ask people their opinions. Remember that you deserve to have your dreams come true.

Question: What is Success?

That's up to you, isn't it? First, you need to understand and clearly define what success is to you. Your values in every aspect of your life will help define the goals for success in each area. Depending on who you are, and the stage of life you are in, success could be that sleek sexy little red sports car, a wealthy lifestyle, a new home for your family. It could be helping your community solve key issues, or being a big sister or big brother and seeing your little sister or brother develop self-esteem and confidence through the relationship. Writing a new novel and having it published or planting a garden that produces food to serve your family in a healthy organic way. It could be losing weight or stopping smoking or finally being able to forgive someone. Perhaps retirement with financial prosperity to travel and enjoy life.

What stage of life are you in? What is success to you?

____

____

____

____

Dreams, goals and aspirations change throughout your life. In retrospect, I have noted major goals and dreams for every 9 year spans. I achieved many of them. My plans for each year bring me closer to the overall ambition, idea or goal I have for my life in the next 5 – 10 years. I had to learn all kinds of information and go through tremendous letting go of bad habits, making the transitions. The things I wanted when I was twenty no longer apply now that I am in my forties. I have focused my life on my values. I expect change; I seek it out and I prepare with all my knowledge for the transitions. It's the exotic soup of excitement!

People seldom understand that change and transition are two different concepts. Change is the external situation, like moving house, changing jobs, someone dying, winning the lottery – often very physical things. Transition on the other hand, is the internal emotional process of understanding, grieving, letting go and being prepared for the new situation. Your results will depend on your character and that means examining the personal stuff.

There are 4 guidelines that seem to help nearly everyone with change and transition. I have heard this from so many sources that I am not sure who is the originator. I will credit the wonderful writer Angeles Arrien. One of my singing teachers wrote a song about these concepts! Be thoughtful here – this could be the one-percent change that affects every transition in your life and leads you on to success.

1) Show up

2) Pay attention

3) Tell the truth

4) Don't be attached to the outcome

How life would change if we applied these simple guidelines: living in the now, being present, showing up fully alert ready for an opportunity or to participate, saying exactly what we mean and letting it go freely. Showing up to your emotions is the most empowering and productive process you will ever have. It will help you live in that space of friendship I talked about earlier.

A short story.

In one of my meditation groups, we were using Goddess cards for inspiration. (Goddess cards are tarot decks that depict archetypes of women seen as goddesses.) I normally do a check in and go around the circle to have participants share any insights or learning from the past week. One woman came in so excited, she could hardly contain herself.

When her turn came . . .

"Oh thank you! You were in my dreams last night!" she said.

I was delighted and curious. "That must have been fun. Do tell!"

She went on to explain that she had been working with visioning and putting pictures on a collage board. Being highly artistic she desired pictures that represented what she wanted to have become reality in her life.

She continued "At one point, for some reason, I got distracted, I stopped putting pictures on the board, and left the collage unfinished. In my dream you appeared with the unfinished collage board and asked me - Would you like to finish this story to create your life, or would you like the Universe to fill it up with something? You have a choice." She woke up startled and wrote down the dream. She finished the collage.

The big trick here is this: If you are willing to clearly define, listen **and walk purposely along the path of your desires;** if you are truly in harmony with your heart and your mind; the infinite intelligence within you and the universe will support you in bringing your dreams into reality . . . with ease and grace

Remember that this is a co-creative endeavour. ACTION is required, so is patience and persistence. When placing Intent to achieve something you must stay alert to the opportunities that present themselves, then know which one is the right one. Great little phrases like "Put the peddle to the metal, and let the rubber hit the road", are great reminders that you are responsible for making the project successful. Also, when you fully hold your energy in the ability to respond with clarity and focus – wow, opportunities really begin to show up.

How quickly success happens is up to you. Are you fully prepared? Have you done your research? Faced your fears? Remember those people that won millions in the lottery and were broke within 1 – 2 years with their family in tatters, no job, no community? What a ride, yet now their lives were in much worse condition. They had no preparation or emotional understanding of the transitions they would need to go through.

I think one of the biggest sources that saps energy and creates emotional mayhem in the mind are all those television commercials and Internet ads. We have been trained by the media and have lost control over our minds. The ads are working like little time bombs in our memory banks. I want, I need, I can have it! It can make you very unhappy, distract, and focus your attention on things that you do not want, also break your financial stability.

I remember once when my ex-partner was fixated on building Greek type columns in the house. The stereo stands were re-designed, he had ideas for a portal for the entrance, the plants needed columns to sit on. Finally one day I sat down with him and watched television. It was right there all over the ads – messages on decorating with roman style columns. I turned to him and said "Do you see all those columns on the ads?" He was so surprised and said "I can't believe I fell for that". You might need to unhook the television, so you can begin to hear yourself.

You know, we all want our lives to be easy and not have to face growth hurdles. Basically, we are a little bit lazy. We have been trained to have it now, the easy lifestyle, the grand vacations. We want with our emotions and justify it with some twisty kind of logic. When I was working with one client on how to align with her goals, teaching some new and different concepts on how to approach her goals, she said, "I just want it the easy way." I turned to her and said, "If you would like to look at your life over the past 11 years and see how hard you have made it, perhaps, this **is** the easy way."

As another client of mine said: "I feel like part of me is screaming and yelling in frustration and beating against a brick wall. The one part of me wants to move forward and transform, and the other wants to say put in familiar comfortable laziness except it's getting less and less comfortable... ARRRRRGGGGGGHHHHHHHHH!!!!" That is what it feels like when you do not have a clear picture of the process, good emotional tools to help yourself go through the transitions and the willingness to burn through the resistance!

On the page 61 you will see a diagram. I call it Steps to Your Goals. You will notice at the lower left, there is a small circle with You, Now, Purpose and a line that goes straight up to Dream, Goal, Vision. On the left hand side are the steps you will need to take to achieve your dream or goal. On the right hand side are spaces for the challenges. The line that runs between them is the line of Resistance, Fears and Self-Sabotage.

I suggest you choose one simple goal you are currently working on. On page 63 I have given an example to work with. State the goal at the bottom circle and know the reason why it is important. Then at the top, put down the dream, goal or vision. On the left hand side, jot down some steps that would help you achieve the goal, on the right side, jot down what your fears or challenges would be for each step. Get to know what your project looks like, get to know

STEPS TO YOUR GOALS

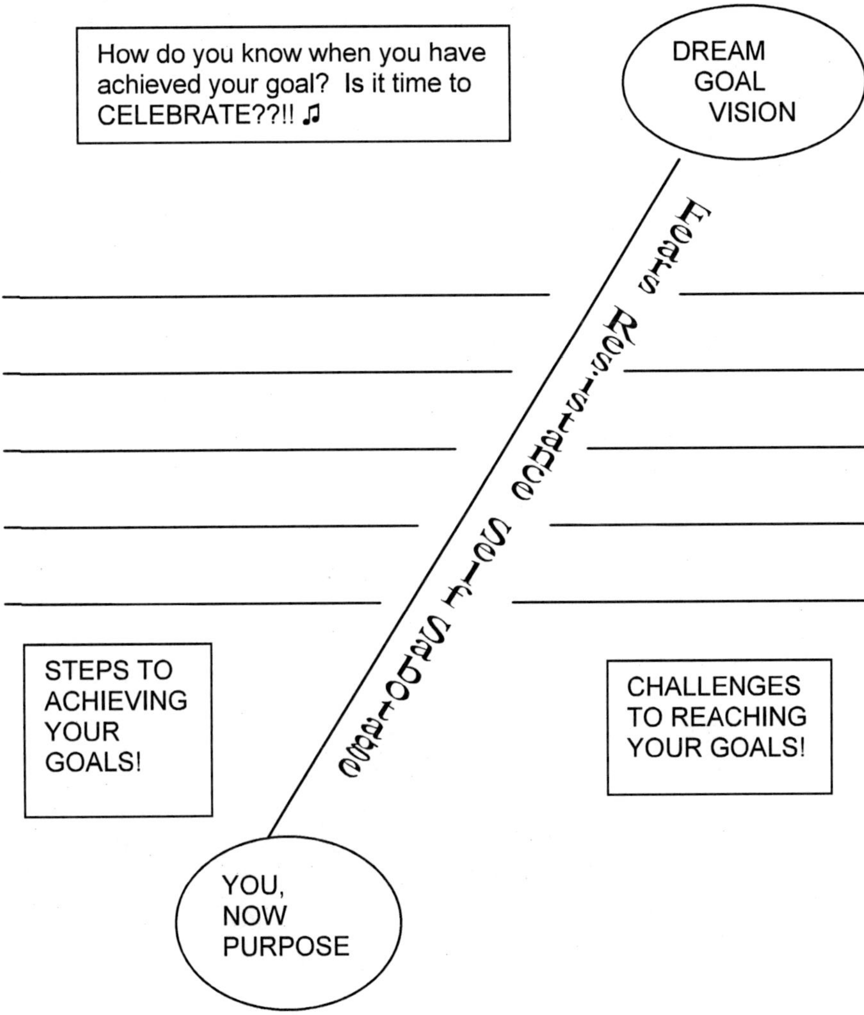

the emotions or ideas that might hold you back. Also, define the end point for your particular goal. What will it look like, feel like, how much money will come in, what will be the moment you know "This is It!" So what is your goal?

____

____

For example: See diagram on page 63

You, Now, Purpose:
Organic garden filled with lavender for Gifts.

Dream Goal Vision:
Sachets of Lavender with little hand made notes of appreciation tied to it for all my friends. JOY

Steps to Achieving Goals:
Research different types of Lavender good for my garden & soil type.
Research different organic fertilizer
Research plants to ward off disease or bugs
Buy the plants and prepare the soil
Dream about the little sachets and notes
etc.

Challenges to Reaching My Goal:
Too many catalogues, lost in all the information
Very expensive for organic products
Which plants to use for pest control or where to plant them.
Special order the plants, the soil is not right, more money.
Fuss, worry, pull weeds, constantly water

For this little goal, when I harvest those exquisite purple blue fragrant lavender flowers and place them in those delightful little sachets with a special note attached, then it is time to celebrate. I can already feel myself enjoying and delighting in seeing them all laid out in their little sachets and giving them to my friends, telling the story about "the garden"! Maybe I would stretch the story a bit and talk about all the bugs and dramatize things. Very funny.

STEPS TO YOUR GOALS

CELEBRATE! ♫ Fresh fruit cobbler with ice cream and a glass of champagne!

Sachets of lavender with hand made notes for all my friends. JOY

STEPS	CHALLENGES
Tend and dream about my garden	Fuss, worry, constant watering
Buy the plants and prepare the soil	Soil is still not right, more dollars
Plants for Disease control	I just don't get it, what to choose
Organic fertilizers	Expensive for organic plants
Research Lavender and soil	Lost, too many catalogues

Organic Garden filled with Lavender. Gift of giving to my friends.

You see, the quick way of moving along your path is having the plan, understanding the fears and challenges, so you can make good decisions, get support and enjoy the journey.

Then achieving your vision requires a celebration! Plan a celebration for achieving your dream or goal or vision. It is so important to acknowledge each step or making decisions along the path, yet make sure you clearly define and accept achieving the goal rather than being a perfectionist and constantly changing things.

Celebration of your goals is a tangible thing to indicate the success of your project. With all your visualizations, preparation and alignment, this is the moment of allowing yourself to thrive, be successful with what you have created and fully embrace having it on every level of your being. When you reach your major goal, celebrate! This is a big part of building self-esteem, increasing trust and friendship, of fueling the fire and being Zesty about your life.

How will you celebrate achieving your goal?

____
____
____
____
____
____

Describe your celebrations in detail or have a little snooze and daydream about your celebration. The more pleasurable emotions you have surrounding the goal, the easier it is to pursue your dream.

Coaching – having some one who totally supports you.

"Coaching, in our experience, is the most effective and expeditious means of helping people build on their strengths and develop to their full potential.
Ruth Brothers, VP Human Resources, Novopharm Limited

On your journey get a good coach, someone with life experience. Find some mentors, have a plan. (A business plan can be a collage or visions board – make it fun!) Be passionate, be persistent, laugh a lot, it will inspire you. Paint pictures in your mind and be juicy with yourself. When you have the space within, the new ideas will leap out at you. Then turn that juice into a plan and start on your path. Review your progress constantly. How well you understand the process and have the skills to make it a prosperous reality will determine the speed of your progress.

No one else lives inside your body with you except the intelligence that holds you together. Well, I certainly hope that is true! If you are stuck in the old habits and think you can just change without doing the transition work OR you apply old techniques to new situations, forget it. Show up being the new you. Walk in the direction you want to go. Make contacts and network. Use the One Minute Active Meditation technique I've shown you here to wash the dirty dishes and take out your mental garbage so you align with where you want to go.

People are amazing; the human spirit is unconquerable. Check if someone has already done or accomplished what you are setting out to do. Figure out how they did it. Learn to ask! You may need to take some courses and get the right training. Stop re-inventing the same wheel. (This is another technique of self-sabotage.) If no one has done what you are attempting to do, then you will need to learn the skills of dream work, visioning and intuition to a higher degree. Remember that if you look around you, everything you see that was created by people was originally someone's vision or dream.

Then you will have achieved with ease and grace . . . SUCCESS!

Reflections:
What is your next goal?
What are the fears or resistance to achieving it?
What action do you want to take?

Ready for the journey?

Chapter 8

EXCURSIONS WITH THE ONE MINUTE ACTIVE MEDITATION TECHNIQUE

"Keep away from people who try to belittle your ambitions. Small people always do that, but the really great make you feel that you, too, can somehow become great."
Mark Twain

Remember I said the One Minute Meditation was an active process. As you move through your daily life, create your world and use this technique, remember that you can simply put your fingertips together, breathe, and ask the Infinite Intelligence within you to expand throughout your body and mind, helping you regain balance, energy and clear the clutter. If you have nothing you want to work on, then simply place intent and say "align me with truth and beauty". Let's get some practice.

Off you go . . . walk down the street and begin noticing what happens in your mind. Listen to the chatter coming up. What is it saying? Hmmm.

Connect your fingertips; breathe two or three full breaths. Instruct your mind to clear the clutter and organize the thoughts. If a particular situation or thought keeps coming up, pay attention! Remember, this is your best friend in here, doing everything you have asked it to do and you are in a co-creative partnership. Your mind will keep repeating all the information and instructions to you (just like your parents did) until you:

A) Write it down – it wants you to remember these things

B) Take the time to fully understand and sort things out

C) Deal with the issue

Keep a pad of paper and pen with you at all times. Thoughts for a new book may pop up, an answer to a difficult question, perhaps some information that you could not quite remember. The more you connect, the more answers to your questions and issues will flow to you.

What about driving the kids to school, or being held up in traffic. Keep your eyes open, touch your fingertips together around the steering wheel and say to yourself. "Please calm and center my mind and body." Breathe in and out.

Let's go to the office – you are sitting in a meeting and losing energy. Minor matters are being discussed at some length. You are tired, drifting off – perhaps a few Maui moments. You need to be present! Put your hands underneath the table, connect your fingertips and say to yourself "Centre and focus my mind and body, energize me." Breathe slowly and deeply. Listen to what is being said in the meeting and feel how you are shifting internally. If you need to do this several times during the meeting, fine. You could be completely energized when it is over.

What about coming home from a busy day of work and you can't stop thinking about a contentious situation. It is driving you crazy, as if the energy of the people and issue is stuck in your mind, going around in circles like a caged rat in a flywheel. Somehow all the energy from the day has thrown you out of balance. Put your fingertips together, breathe, close your eyes and place intent. Ask the infinite intelligence within to please release all the energy from the situation and from the day. Clear all the emotional clutter and associations from your past experiences. Imagine the heavy energy like a dense cloud around you, perhaps inside of you, and see it dissolving. Then see a pearly beautiful light filling you up from the inside out.

Decisions. Sometimes we are faced with doing what is right or what is easy. I know for myself that what appeared easy at the time, often led to difficulties later. The right answer came from that deeper inner place. Making decisions can seem overwhelming at times - which way to go, what is the best solution, how will that play out for the months or years ahead. From financial planning to changing jobs, what to wear on a date, to choosing a new car, defining what is important and aligning with that. Once you have built a foundation of trust within, I would encourage you to ask that infinite intelligence within for that decision – and try it out. Get a track record and build some trust. So, put your fingertips together, eyes closed, breathing. "Infinite Intelligence within, please clear all the clutter of my thoughts around this issue. Help me understand the way or choices that is the best for me." Write it down, then go through your logical process and compare the two responses.

Healing. If you take a little time every day to feel juicy, loved, cherished inside of you, illness will not come knocking on your door that often. Wear yourself down with bad habits, lack of care and you could have dis-ease as a constant companion.

Here's a suggestion: First thing when you wake up in the morning and last thing at night before you go to sleep, put your fingertips together, breathe and remember the most beautiful feeling of love in your heart. Expand that feeling through your entire being. There are thousands of memories or daily acts of kindness that happen every day. Simply focus on one and connect with your heart in that loving embrace. Place intent "Infinite Intelligence please increase the energy in my body to be whole, healthy, filled with beauty and truth." Notice what happens.

Going a little deeper?

Old painful memories. From childhood onward, we have been trained to obey authority outside of our self. "NO" has been drilled in to our minds and hearts and ways of being. When I was working on some deep personal issues, one that came up was self hate. I was shocked - where did that come from. How could I hate myself? Then the memories started flooding in and I understood. The lesson I learned was that I had to take my personal power, my personal authority back to myself. "Infinite Intelligence within, please expand within me and help me dissolve, clear and forgive all the patterns of self hate I hold in my body, memory and energy. Please help me fill up with light, truth and beauty." What happened was astonishing. My body jerked so hard it felt like something cracked, then flooding warmth spread through me so fast I felt like I was burning up. My energy was zooming. Think about how much energy is trapped inside of you. Give yourself permission to free the past.

Public speaking. I have helped many people learn to speak dynamically and go through the process of understanding the stories created by their fears using this one minute technique. No amount of imagining people seated in their underwear helped my self-confidence! The fears were there as information, as stories, and looking at the information provided the clues as to how to deal with the stories.

Put your fingertips together, breathe, close your eyes and imagine you are in a room about to speak to a group of people. Ask the infinite intelligence to bring up all the thoughts or fears so you can write them down and deal with them. Listen. Hold yourself steady while you wait and listen. You want to know the information so you can deal with it. It is only the unknown or wild imaginings that create those dreadful fears and fantasies.

Then, after writing down the stories, begin by asking for forgiveness for the negative emotions you are holding on to. Every time you are criticizing someone else or yourself – it is often your own deep feelings of lack of self-esteem. You are scared and perhaps scarred from past experiences. Hold your heart, ask for the truth to release these critical thoughts. Ask the infinite intelligence to expand within you and bring the clear warm light of truth in to all those cold negative critical thoughts and stories. Ask your body and mind to release the stories that have shut down on your creativity, trust and joy of sharing. See yourself surrounded in a gentle circle of light that pulls the old thoughts and everything associated with them, out of your body, dissolving the tension. Then see and imagine that space filling up with beautiful colors, roses, something special, just for you. Give yourself permission to explore what you feel.

How about a learning tour? This is a seated meditation where you have an imaginary conversation with someone you truly respect. This could be a teacher, mentor, therapist, and meditation group leader or good friend. In your imagination, create a visual whereby you go for a walk with this person and have a conversation.

Imagine you have a question that you would really like help with. They would be more than willing to help you understand the situation and come to a good answer. Allow every impression; notice the comfort and joy of being in their presence. Feel the warmth and trust of this meeting. Laugh and smile at your own misunderstandings and feel intelligence and understanding flood through your being. When you are done, thank them. Thank your self. Come back and be present in the room. Review everything you have felt or thought during your conversation, even if the other person has simply listened. You could even use this visualization with a good friend or relative who has died, something to heal the heart in comfort.

Reflections:
What challenges are you currently faced with?
How could you apply this one minute technique on a daily basis?
What benefits do you get from daily practice?

Ready to find out more about you?

Chapter 9

NINE QUICK STEPS

"Once again,
I saw the dazzling stars
shine in my heart,
like glistening diamonds
nestled around a magnificent Ruby."
Alannah Jantzen

In chapter 6, I went into detail on building the foundation for the One Minute Active Meditation. Yet, people have often said to me, if I could just listen to your voice, it would make it so much easier. Therefore, the CD in the back of this book specifically takes you through a 30 minute guided meditation to build that foundation. Un-cluttering your mind with the sounds of the Tibetan singing bowl and then connecting to the light exactly as described here in this book.

Here is Building the Framework in 9 simple steps. I invite you to dance in the beauty of your soul.

1) Make a date with yourself!

2) Choose a quiet safe space with a comfy chair. Turn off the telephones, televisions, computers, and all gadgets, especially the clock and please take off your wristwatch! Put a Do Not Disturb sign on the door.

3) Tell yourself that you are going to sit down, you will be closing your eyes and you want to connect within. You want to connect with this infinite intelligence in your

4) Close your eyes. Close your inner invisible eyelids. Make your eyes heavy.

5) Put all your fingertips on one hand together and all the fingertips on the other hand together. Place one hand on each leg or chair arm. Feel the sensations.

6) Breathe slowly and deeply into your belly.

7) Instruct your brain/mind to organize all the thoughts. "Infinite Intelligence, un-clutter my mind. Put all the information in the right categories and places, neat and tidy. Numbers, names, dates, everything ordered, so I can retrieve it whenever I need or want to, easily and effortlessly. I'll give you 5 minutes. At the end of those 5 minutes, I would like it completed and my mind calm so it can prepare to do other fun activities. Thank you! Begin now".

8) Visualization – greet the morning sun rising over the ocean!

9) Ask the infinite intelligence to expand within you so that you may know it in every cell of your being. Stay with that feeling for a few minutes. Give thanks.

The One Minute Active Meditation Technique is:

1) Put your fingertips together.

2) Close your eyes (if it is safe to do so).

3) Take several deep breaths.

4) Ask or place intent for the Infinite Intelligence within you to expand and do ________________ (whatever is needed), in one minute.

By putting your fingertips together, breathing and placing intent, you are connecting to the guided meditation and all the good feelings generated in the meditation. If you give your inner wisdom a time frame of one minute to accomplish the task, you inner wisdom knows to do it quickly.

It is very helpful if you can be quiet when you make the request as this does take energy. Doing deep breathing will be fuel for the body and systems to go to work.

Enjoy!

Conclusion:

We have been gifted with a highly complex system we call our body/mind, infused with this Infinite Intelligence of our spirit/soul. In this book I have given you a clear path of understanding how to connect with the living presence, Infinite intelligence within and why doing so will connect you with a Zest and life force that is reflected in the health of your body and clarity of your mind.

When you make a deep pact of friendship within, you will begin to build the trust, courage and self esteem to carry you through all of life's challenges (Spiritual pushups) for a life that can be filled with more ease and grace.

Mother Teresa said " . . . in the end, it is never between you and them, it is between you and God. So do it anyway."

I understand the word God to mean the Infinite Intelligence within you and me and within every living thing on this planet and in the cosmos. That creative force that gives zest to life. If you want to truly understand your self and gift your self with the most precious relationship you will ever have, then I highly recommend meditation to develop the relationship within. From the amazing abilities of the mind in to the depth of knowing the heart – it is the journey of a lifetime.

Remember that the life you seek of joy, calm, health, or success is with the knowledge and connection within. It's all within you. It is an inside job.

So, never wait for the meditation police to give you a ticket!
Put your fingertips together and follow your Bliss -
Connect with your Zest!

Blessings on the journey of life:

May your heart radiate Joy,

May your eyes glisten with Beauty,

May your lips bless the world with your Song.

Alannah Jantzen

The beginning.

Further reading:

Heart Math Institute
http://www.heartmath.org
The store offers many books on their leading edge research. Get to know your heart.

Angeles Arrien
The Nine Muses – A mythological path to creativity
Anthropologist, educator, and award-winning author. I have enjoyed her books and passion for life through a creative, mythological approach.

Gertrud Hirschi
Mudras – Yoga in your hands
Gertrud teaches yoga in accordance with the latest medical findings. Her book Mudras gives a clear description of the different systems – Ayurveda, Chakras, Acupressure, Reflex zones, Meridians, Planetary classification, palmistry and yoga mudras - and how these are activated through the hands.

William Bridges
Managing Transitions – Making the Most of Change.
An easy read to understanding change and transitions for business.

Marc Allen
Visionary Business – Entrepreneur's guide to Success.
A great story, solid business insights and inspiration for the fledgling entrepreneur.

Divorce Care program
Check out your local churches. Or go to http://www.divorcecare.org

Bruce Lipton Ph.D
The Biology Of Belief: Unleashing The Power Of Consciousness, Matter And Miracles
A renaissance in Cell Biology now provides the cutting edge science - real science - to prove how holistic health therapies work. A former medical school professor and research scientist, his experiments, and that of other leading-edge scientists, have examined in great detail the processes by which cells receive information.

His Holiness the Dalai Lama with Howard Cutler M. D.
The Art of Happiness – A handbook for Living
Understanding compassion for self and others in simple language with wonderful heart felt stories. You can feel the love shine through his words.

Eckhardt Tolle
The Power of Now – A guide to spiritual enlightenment.
This is an excellent book meant to be read and understood in a slow deliberate fashion. Otherwise your ego will simply twist you in to new stories.

Keith Yamashita & Sandra Spataro
Unstuck – A tool for yourself, your team and your world.
A smart practical guide to turn to for inspiration and immediate solutions. Based on experience working with teams and individuals in IBM, Sony, Hewlett-Packard, Nike etc.

About the Author - Alannah Jantzen

Inspirational Speaker and Coach, Alannah Jantzen blends traditional wisdom with modern business practices in a joyous process of connect with your Zest creativity. Her seminars are dynamic expressions of spirit filled connection with life purpose and meaning.

Alannah also writes and records meditations and specialized commute and learn programs for businesses. She has over 20 years in holistic integrative health. Her formal training includes both Registered Massage Therapy (retired), and Certified Clinical Hypnotherapy. In 1995, she began cross cultural teachings from the Inka (Peru) and First Nations, along with the Foundation for Shamanic Studies. Training in coaching, meditation, yoga, energy work, singing, sound and light healing have complemented her work activities and love of life long learning.

Originally from Vancouver, B.C., Canada, Alannah has led an artistic and adventuresome journey in life. From working as a massage therapist in the heli-skiing industry, bicycling 3,000 miles in Europe, sailing 12,000 miles in the Caribbean and Central America, to guiding sacred sites tours to Sedona, Arizona, U.S.A. Artistically, she has crafted hand frame drums, community drums and recorded two CD's – Flow Spirit Flow and Work of the Spirit.

To contact Alannah for speaking engagements, seminars, or coaching:
1-604-420-7712
Email: ajantzen@telus.net
Website: www.withzest.com